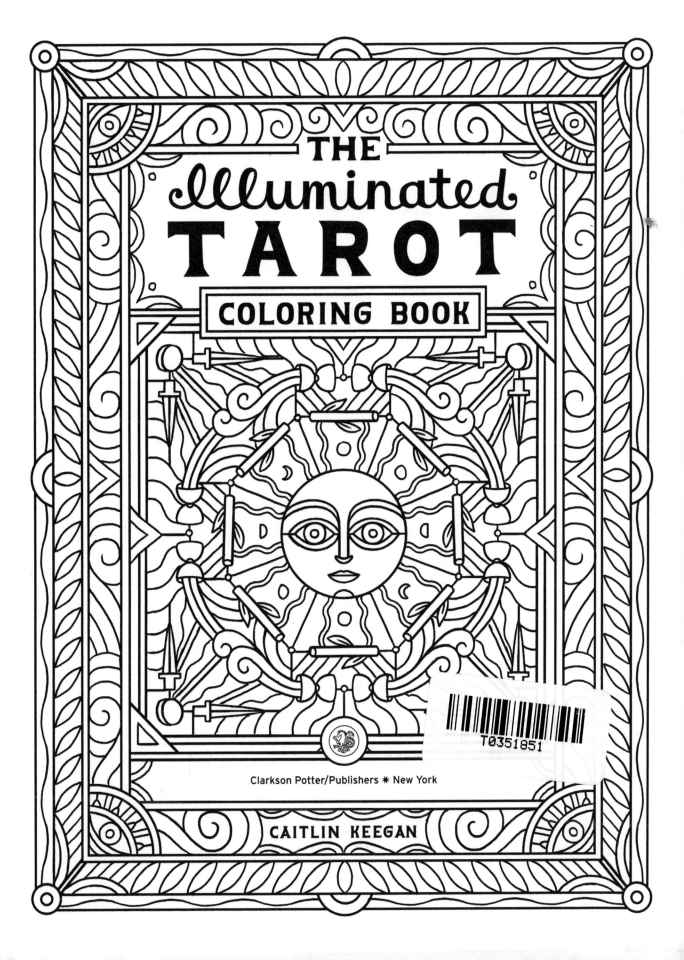

THE
Illuminated
TAROT
COLORING BOOK

Clarkson Potter/Publishers ✳ New York

CAITLIN KEEGAN

INTRODUCTION

One aspect of tarot history that has always captured my attention is its connection to playing cards. So much is unknown about the precise origin of tarot as we know it, but we do know that tarot and playing cards were used interchangeably in places all over the world as far back as the ninth century. I loved the idea of bringing the two formats together in a fully illustrated deck with multiple uses. *The Illuminated Tarot* card deck follows the framework of a fifty-two-card playing card deck but folds in tarot's Major Arcana archetypes. Each of the Major Arcana cards in *The Illuminated Tarot* card deck combines the symbolism of two traditional tarot cards: one Major and one Minor Arcana card.

Tarot imagery is a rich resource for thoughtful, introspective analysis because an individual's interpretation of an image can change depending on context. The way we interpret an image six weeks or six years from now may differ from how we read it today, life experiences shift our perspective. This is where the magic of tarot lies. The descriptions in this coloring book reveal what I had in mind when I created the cards, but there is no "correct" interpretation of these images. I hope you will take notes in the margins on your interpretations and use the descriptions here to support and expand upon your own intuitive understanding.

About *The Illuminated Tarot*

DECK INTRODUCTION

As mentioned above, *The Illuminated Tarot* card deck incorporates tarot's twenty-two Major Arcana archetypes into the structure of a traditional fifty-two-card playing card deck. Each of the Major Arcana cards illustrated here has double meaning, as the art also represents a Minor Arcana archetype.

The Illuminated Tarot follows the same court structure as playing cards, swapping Jacks for tarot's Pages. The Knights that would be found in a traditional seventy-eight-card tarot deck are not included. The deck also includes one Joker, which corresponds to tarot's Fool, for a total of fifty-three cards.

TAROT SYMBOLISM

The Illuminated Tarot uses the suit structure of playing cards (clubs, diamonds, hearts, spades) and ascribes each to a traditional tarot suit. You can use the number and other suit associations below to add depth to your intuitive reading of the images and cards as a whole.

SUITS

Suit	Tarot Suit	Theme	Element	Cognitive Function
♣ CLUBS	Wands	Passion and Creativity	Fire	Intuition
♦ DIAMONDS	Coins or Pentacles	The Physical World	Earth	Sensation
♥ HEARTS	Cups	Emotion and Intuition	Water	Feeling
♠ SPADES	Swords	Reason and Intellect	Air	Thinking

NUMBERS

Ace (1)	a seed, a beginning, clarity	6	cooperation, community, communication
2	duality, dialogue, choice	7	possibility, discovery, spirituality
3	creation, family, group dynamics	8	cycles, patterns, repetition
4	stability, structure, foundation	9	idealism, expectation, attainment
5	change, imbalance, division	10	resolution, completion, advancement

COURT CARDS

Court cards can refer to character traits, people who have these traits, or energetic influences. Court cards are not indicators of gender; anyone can take on or be represented by the attributes of Jacks, Queens, and Kings. (A traditional seventy-eight-card tarot deck also includes Knights, but *The Illuminated Tarot* does not.) The court cards are placed here in ascending playing card order, but you can decide your own hierarchy, if any.

JACKS	Associated with inexperience	Students or apprentices
QUEENS	Open-minded and intuitive	Leaders or mentors
KINGS	Rule-based and methodical	Leaders or mentors

COLOR PALETTES AND INSPIRATION

Each suit in *The Illuminated Tarot* card deck has its own defined color palette. Some colors are present in all four palettes, and The Joker/Fool card incorporates all the deck colors.

You can create palettes intuitively, but color inspiration is everywhere if you need it. Some places to look for inspiration include photographs, interior settings, your own closet, or a piece of artwork or a textile you love. Take photos on a walk around your neighborhood. Go to a museum and see what objects or artwork you feel drawn to. Scroll through the photos on your phone. Flip through books on your shelves or in a used bookstore. Observe your surroundings with an eye toward color and see what inspiration emerges.

The color palette for *The Illuminated Tarot* card deck was inspired by early twentieth-century textile designer E.A. Séguy, who used unexpected combinations of saturated color in his work. The goal was to evoke a vibrant, printed textile and to give each suit a specific emotional tone. The Clubs suit, for example, represents passion and corresponds to the element of fire, so the palette feels warm and sunny. The Spades suit corresponds to reason, intellect, and the element of air, so the color palette feels serious and thoughtful. You can read more about suit correspondences on the previous page and see if these inspire your ideas about color.

COLOR EXPLORATION

There are, of course, no rules, but if you'd like to choose color palettes for your coloring pages—one for each of the four suits or one for the whole deck—you can use this page to experiment with different color combinations.

♣
CLUBS

○○○○○○○
○○○○○○○
○○○○○○○
○○○○○○○
○○○○○○○

♦
DIAMONDS

○○○○○○○
○○○○○○○
○○○○○○○
○○○○○○○
○○○○○○○

♠
SPADES

○○○○○○○
○○○○○○○
○○○○○○○
○○○○○○○
○○○○○○○

♥
HEARTS

○○○○○○○
○○○○○○○
○○○○○○○
○○○○○○○
○○○○○○○

JOKER / THE FOOL

○○○○○○○○○○○○○○

JOKER ✳ THE FOOL

Freedom, fearlessness

The Fool marks the beginning of a journey. In fact, tarot is often referred to as The Fool's Journey, with the subsequent Major Arcana cards representing different aspects of human experience and development. The journey ahead will have its ups and downs, and we will learn and change along the way. At the start, we must trust the process and begin with a sense of openness and wonder.

QUICK READING

Zero is the mathematical balance point between positive and negative; it is associated with a womb or a void—potential or nothingness.

+

The Joker is depicted as a comedic, trickster-type figure associated with play, childlike enthusiasm, and a disregard for established rules and norms.

=

The Fool is all about possibility and potential. Anything can happen.

NOTES

ACE OF CLUBS ✳ STRENGTH

Overcoming desire, building trust, courage

In early tarot decks, the Strength card was illustrated with Hercules killing the Nemean Lion. In modern decks, the card has less to do with outward displays of force and instead represents inner strength, encompassing qualities of faith, loyalty, and patience. The lion indicates an inner wildness that can either be tamed or allowed to run free when the situation calls for it. Courage is the result of an inner balance: a healthy attitude toward fear and confidence that comes from knowing oneself.

QUICK READING

Ace/One signifies clarity and new beginnings.

+

Clubs represent passion and creativity and correspond to the element of fire.

=

This image combines the clarity of the Ace with the courage and patience required to tame a wild animal. A tamed lion symbolizes controlled instincts.

NOTES

TWO OF CLUBS

A passionate conversation or debate

Here, an intense dialogue creates friction like two sticks rubbed together to spark fire. What we do with the fire and how much it progresses depends on whether we intended to start it in the first place. Most traditional interpretations of this card involve a feeling of discontent that the fight—and the sense of purpose that came with it—has come to an end.

QUICK READING

Two signifies duality: a dialogue or choice.

+

Clubs represent passion and creativity and correspond to the element of fire.

=

The image traditionally signifies an intensity between two entities and the idea of finding meaning in the process rather than focusing on the result.

NOTES

THREE OF CLUBS

Efforts rewarded, success in business

The Three of Clubs represents success that comes from planning and strategy. Once the basic groundwork is laid or a home base is established, a new project or experience is free to take on a life of its own. This card is about the passion and willpower required at the earliest stages of creating something new.

QUICK READING

Three signifies creation, as well as family or group dynamics.

+

Clubs represent passion and creativity and correspond to the element of fire.

=

The image illustrates a foundation built with hard work and intention. With a safe home base, we can move beyond our basic needs and focus on learning, creation, and growth.

NOTES

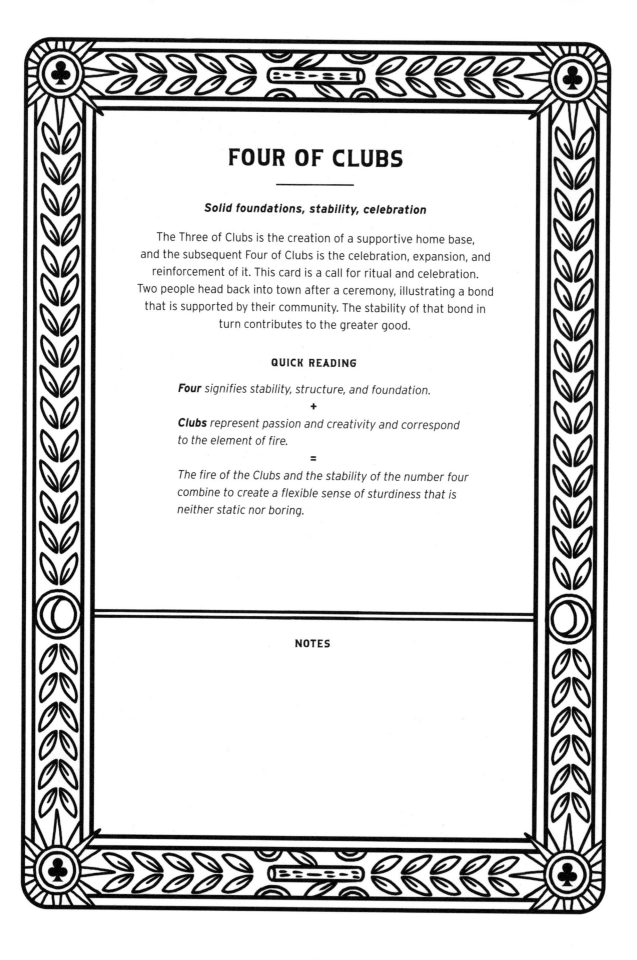

FOUR OF CLUBS

Solid foundations, stability, celebration

The Three of Clubs is the creation of a supportive home base, and the subsequent Four of Clubs is the celebration, expansion, and reinforcement of it. This card is a call for ritual and celebration. Two people head back into town after a ceremony, illustrating a bond that is supported by their community. The stability of that bond in turn contributes to the greater good.

QUICK READING

Four signifies stability, structure, and foundation.

+

Clubs represent passion and creativity and correspond to the element of fire.

=

The fire of the Clubs and the stability of the number four combine to create a flexible sense of sturdiness that is neither static nor boring.

NOTES

FIVE OF CLUBS ✴ THE DEVIL

Temptation, attachment, control

In Buddhist, Hindu, and other philosophies, attachment is considered the source of all suffering. The Devil traditionally signifies materialism or attachment. The figures here are trapped by chains and fire— a combination of the intense conflict indicated by the Five of Clubs and The Devil's ability to confine, control, and limit our perspective.

QUICK READING

Five signifies imbalance and change.

+

Clubs represent passion and creativity and correspond to the element of fire.

=

Fives may involve struggle or the need for a new strategy. This card could signify an urge to control or a feeling of being controlled, whether it be a person, habit, situation, or commitment.

NOTES

SIX OF CLUBS ✳ THE TOWER

A revelation or drastic shift in perspective

The Tower represents a moment of realization. A goal we have
been working toward is not turning out as expected. Imagine building
a tower on a shaky, uneven foundation. Sometimes starting over is
the only safe way forward. Once truth is acknowledged, we can
progress in a more honest and informed way.

QUICK READING

Six signifies cooperation, community, and
communication.

+

Clubs represent passion and creativity and correspond
to the element of fire.

=

*This card requires us to see through our own delusions,
asking whether there is tension in our communication
with others or if dread stems from something we have
not fully acknowledged.*

NOTES

SEVEN OF CLUBS

Vigilance, a struggle to stay ahead

The Seven of Clubs can refer to a conflict—internal or external—that presents us with a challenge and a chance for growth. This challenge may not involve conflict with another person or group; rather, it could be a creative or spiritual conflict. This card also asks us to examine the role of competition in our lives.

QUICK READING

Seven signifies possibility, discovery, and spirituality.

\+

Clubs represent passion and creativity and correspond to the element of fire.

\=

Do each of the beavers in the image need to build their own dam, or could they combine forces? We should examine what we have to gain or lose by competing. How can this conflict provide an opportunity for discovery, regardless of the outcome?

NOTES

EIGHT OF CLUBS

Repetition, swift movement to create stability

The Eight of Clubs is about energy and focus: knowing exactly what needs to be done and doing it. When we feel passionate about something, making it happen feels effortless. An archer may appear to hit their target effortlessly, but it only looks that way because of their previous effort and practice. When we pull the Eight of Clubs, we are ready to put our training to good use.

QUICK READING

Eight *signifies patterns, cycles, and repetition.*

+

Clubs *represent passion and creativity and correspond to the element of fire.*

=

As the bird pictured here builds a nest, it works quickly and efficiently—it understands the underlying pattern within the nest structure. A sturdy nest can be accomplished with a strong will and a thoughtful mind.

NOTES

NINE OF CLUBS ✳ THE SUN

Clarity, simplicity, new life

The Sun is about "shedding light" on things that seem unclear or uncertain. Apollo, the sun god in Greek mythology, is also the god of truth. As the source of life on earth, The Sun encompasses play, freedom, and physicality as well. The Sun is in direct contrast to The Moon, which is introspective and mysterious. In traditional tarot and alchemical symbolism, The Sun is associated with masculinity, and The Moon with femininity. These associations are tied to the mythological brother-sister pairing of Apollo (Sun) and Artemis (Moon).

QUICK READING

Nine signifies expectation and idealism.

+

Clubs represent passion and creativity and correspond to the element of fire.

=

Since this card is a combination of fiery Clubs and the idealistic number nine, it has an exuberant, optimistic, and extroverted energy.

NOTES

TEN OF CLUBS

A responsibility or burden

The Ten of Clubs is a reminder to pace ourselves to avoid burnout.
Are we working too hard or taking on too much? Are we moving at
an unsustainable pace? We have reached the end of a cycle, and in the
process of getting there, we have accumulated more than we need.
Before we can enter a new phase, we should assess what to bring
along and what to leave behind.

QUICK READING

Ten signifies resolution and completion.

+

Clubs represent passion and creativity and correspond
to the element of fire.

=

*The Ten of Clubs may signal a creative project that has
exceeded its original scope or a relationship that has
become too intense. Though ten signifies completion,
the sticks in the image are a weight and an obstacle.
The key to moving forward is to define what is essential.*

NOTES

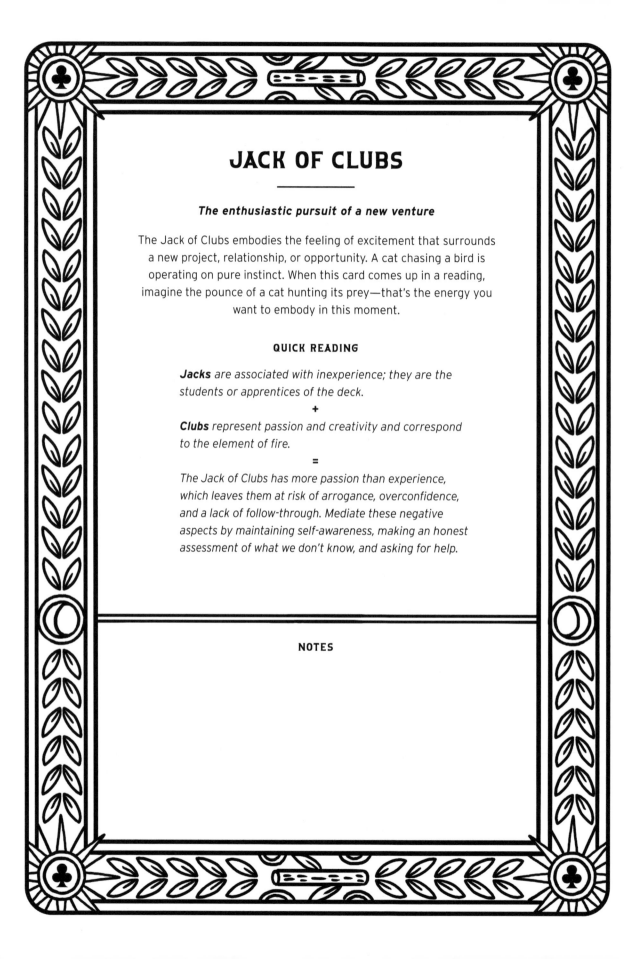

JACK OF CLUBS

The enthusiastic pursuit of a new venture

The Jack of Clubs embodies the feeling of excitement that surrounds a new project, relationship, or opportunity. A cat chasing a bird is operating on pure instinct. When this card comes up in a reading, imagine the pounce of a cat hunting its prey—that's the energy you want to embody in this moment.

QUICK READING

Jacks are associated with inexperience; they are the students or apprentices of the deck.

+

Clubs represent passion and creativity and correspond to the element of fire.

=

The Jack of Clubs has more passion than experience, which leaves them at risk of arrogance, overconfidence, and a lack of follow-through. Mediate these negative aspects by maintaining self-awareness, making an honest assessment of what we don't know, and asking for help.

NOTES

QUEEN OF CLUBS

Confidence, strength

The Queen of Clubs is the personification of The Sun's fiery optimism and Strength's inner fortitude. She is warm, magnetic, and self-assured. Those who embody this card project confidence, while also motivating and inspiring others. As natural leaders, these individuals also possess open-mindedness, passion, and creativity. They know when to show restraint and when to be vulnerable; they connect deeply with others while maintaining their own unique perspective.

QUICK READING

Queens *are open-minded and intuitive leaders or mentors.*

+

Clubs *represent passion and creativity and correspond to the element of fire.*

=

Here, the Queen of Clubs projects confidence and warmth. She is surrounded by a dense thicket of sunflowers—symbols of joy, power, and positivity.

NOTES

KING OF CLUBS ✶ THE MAGICIAN

Skill, transformation

The concept of transformation comes up often in the tarot, but The Magician specifically addresses transformation that is within our control. When this card shows up, we can also reflect on the importance of intention. Sometimes we have all the necessary tools at our disposal and just need to figure out what we want.

QUICK READING

Kings are rule-based and methodical leaders or mentors.

+

Clubs represent passion and creativity and correspond to the element of fire.

=

This card represents someone who uses their passion and skill to create alchemy. The King of Clubs shares The Magician's warmth and motivation to make significant, positive change.

NOTES

ACE OF DIAMONDS ✳ THE WORLD

Peace, travel, open-mindedness

In her book *Seventy-Eight Degrees of Wisdom*, divinatory tarot expert Rachel Pollack refers to The World as the "unconscious known consciously." This card represents the freedom to live honestly and with a solid understanding of our place on Earth. When our inner and outer selves align, we feel at home anywhere.

QUICK READING

Ace/One signifies clarity and new beginnings.

+

Diamonds represent the physical world and correspond to the element of earth.

=

If we think of Aces as seeds, this Ace of Diamonds is fully embedded in the earth and will take on the strongest form its environment will allow. This card is a reminder that our growth is dependent on our ecosystem and relationships.

NOTES

TWO OF DIAMONDS ✳ THE HIGH PRIESTESS

Juggling, multitasking

The earliest surviving tarot decks refer to The High Priestess as La Papesse, or female pope. The High Priestess transcends binaries to serve a higher purpose. Similarly, the Two of Diamonds represents a dialogue between interdependent, contradicting aspects, like light and shadow. This card represents tolerance for ambiguity and the wisdom that comes from knowing that multiple points of view can be valid.

QUICK READING

Two signifies duality: a dialogue or a choice.

+

Diamonds represent the physical world and correspond to the element of earth.

=

The figure is comprised of two columns, light and dark, similar to the Yin and Yang symbol in Chinese philosophy: two opposite, yet interdependent components that form a whole.

NOTES

THREE OF DIAMONDS

Craftsmanship, successful collaboration, admiration

Some goals can't be accomplished alone. This card is a reminder to ask for help when needed and to appreciate the unique skills and abilities of those around us. This card is also about craft, spirituality, and the meaning behind the collaborative work we do. Three collaborators step back to admire the work they've completed. Pausing to appreciate the work we've done is an important part of the creation process.

QUICK READING

Three signifies creation, as well as family or group dynamics.

+

Diamonds represent the physical world and correspond to the element of earth.

=

Both the Three of Diamonds and the Eight of Diamonds refer explicitly to work. While the Eight of Diamonds represents a solitary process, this card is specifically about collaborative work.

NOTES

FOUR OF DIAMONDS

Hesitation to help others, preoccupation with material possessions

This card is about not holding on tightly to our material possessions. We could spin the idea of stinginess into the positively connotated thriftiness or, simply, caution. Setting boundaries can be positive but it is important not to close ourselves off entirely. We lose some of our freedom when we exert too much control.

QUICK READING

Four signifies stability, structure, and foundation.

+

Diamonds represent the physical world and correspond to the element of earth.

=

A figure peers out cautiously from behind a locked door. Their crown and the garden behind them indicate wealth and security. Their expression is one of fearfulness or concern—they are locked in and locked out at the same time.

NOTES

FIVE OF DIAMONDS ✳ THE HIEROPHANT

Tradition, spiritual authority, deception

The word *hierophant* comes from ancient Greek and refers to a
spiritual leader who acts as an intermediary between humanity and a
higher power. In early Italian tarot decks, this Major Arcana card was
called The Pope. Spiritual leaders are assumed to have access
to knowledge that their followers do not, so authority and deception
can be two sides of the same coin.

QUICK READING

Five signifies imbalance and change.

+

Diamonds represent the physical world and correspond
to the element of earth.

=

*The number five suggests imbalance, perhaps indicating
that putting blind faith in a teacher, mentor, or
spiritual tradition may create instability. When seeking
mentorship, be careful around those who speak in
absolutes.*

NOTES

SIX OF DIAMONDS

Charity, harmony, cooperation

When this card appears in a reading, we could think about the metaphor of "bringing something to the table." What do we have to contribute? What assistance do we receive from others? This card conveys joyful sharing, seeing the good in other people, and relying on others. Everyone is happily contributing what they can, and the whole is greater than the individual parts.

QUICK READING

Six signifies cooperation, community, and communication.

+

Diamonds represent the physical world and correspond to the element of earth.

=

What do cooperation, community, and communication mean in relation to the physical world? This card is about dependability, generosity, and balancing resources among your friends and neighbors.

NOTES

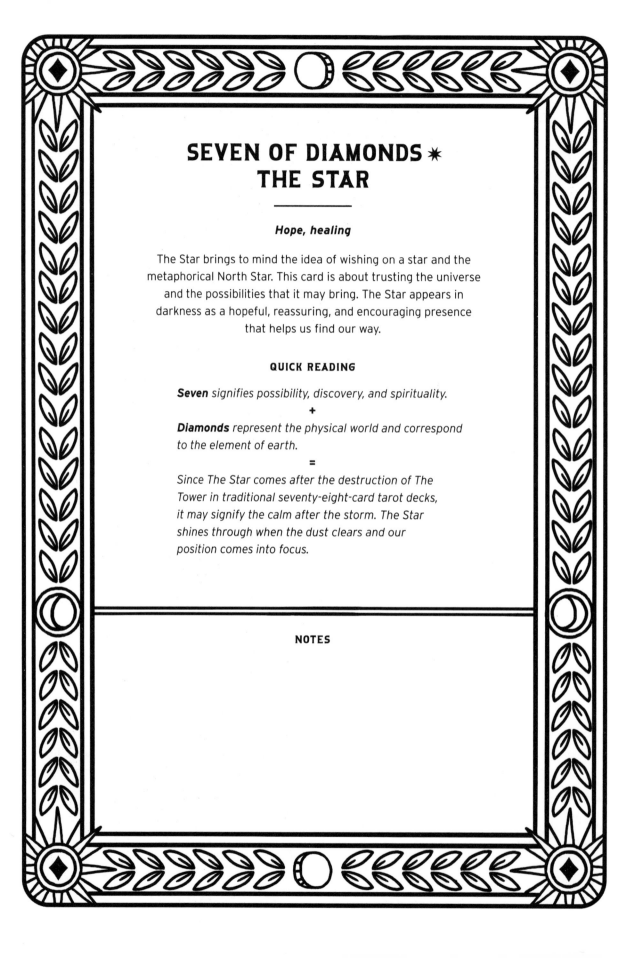

SEVEN OF DIAMONDS ✳ THE STAR

Hope, healing

The Star brings to mind the idea of wishing on a star and the metaphorical North Star. This card is about trusting the universe and the possibilities that it may bring. The Star appears in darkness as a hopeful, reassuring, and encouraging presence that helps us find our way.

QUICK READING

Seven *signifies possibility, discovery, and spirituality.*

+

Diamonds *represent the physical world and correspond to the element of earth.*

=

Since The Star comes after the destruction of The Tower in traditional seventy-eight-card tarot decks, it may signify the calm after the storm. The Star shines through when the dust clears and our position comes into focus.

NOTES

EIGHT OF DIAMONDS

Comfort achieved through work and persistence

The Eight of Diamonds is the craftsmanship card. It encompasses the feeling of being fully absorbed in work. Quilting symbolizes the creation of something functional and meaningful, and the idea of getting lost in a creative process. Quilting also connects to tradition and the continuity of shared skills over generations, so this work may also have spiritual significance.

QUICK READING

Eight signifies patterns, cycles, and repetition.

+

Diamonds represent the physical world and correspond to the element of earth.

=

The combination of the hard-working Diamonds and the repetition imbued in the number eight prompts the idea of practicing a craft and perhaps losing ourselves in meaningful work.

NOTES

NINE OF DIAMONDS ✳ THE HERMIT

Sacrifice without regret, self-care

This card asks us to observe our own thoughts and feelings,
free from outside influences, and to enjoy our own company.
The image might bring to mind a hermit crab, but the animal shown
here is a nautilus. The inside of a nautilus shell is a logarithmic spiral.
Spirals are symbolically connected to the moon, labyrinths,
death and rebirth, growth, and evolution.

QUICK READING

Nine signifies expectation and idealism.

+

Diamonds represent the physical world and correspond
to the element of earth.

=

*In traditional seventy-eight-card tarot decks, the Nine of
Diamonds and The Hermit both represent solitude and
self-discipline. They traditionally convey wisdom, ease,
and security.*

NOTES

TEN OF DIAMONDS

A choice of security over risk, enjoyment of wealth

The Ten of Diamonds is the card of healthy, harmonious relationships and stable situations. As the saying goes, "as above, so below"—there is synchronicity and order, and all is right with the universe. This card represents everyday happiness: being content with what we have and enjoying our day-to-day life. The Ten of Diamonds asks what makes us feel complete. It also reminds us to step back and acknowledge the wealth we have in terms of family, friendships, or community support.

QUICK READING

Ten signifies resolution and completion.

+

Diamonds represent the physical world and correspond to the element of earth.

=

This card, which may represent a family or, more generally, intergenerational harmony, is about sharing knowledge and experiences. The image conveys a continuity of experience that creates a stable community.

NOTES

JACK OF DIAMONDS

Fascination, wonder, scholarship

The Jack of Diamonds learns about the world around them
by observing and drawing it. They appear to be deep in thought,
captivated by their subject. Working diligently brings them a sense
of greater possibility. Since the Diamonds suit also represents
business or finance, this card could indicate learning on the job
or learning to manage money.

QUICK READING

Jacks are associated with inexperience; they are
the students or apprentices of the deck.

+

Diamonds represent the physical world and correspond
to the element of earth.

=

Consider what it means to be a student of the Earth.
Maybe we are learning to be more grounded or to
appreciate the world as it is instead of how we wish
it would be.

NOTES

QUEEN OF DIAMONDS

---

*A bond between the internal and external,
mastery—not control—of nature*

The Queen of Diamonds feels at home anywhere, and in the
image it is difficult to see where the Queen ends and nature begins.
As an adaptive observer, she blends with her surroundings and
makes those around her feel comfortable. This figure embodies
practicality, self-awareness, and ingenuity.

QUICK READING

Queens *are open-minded and intuitive leaders or*
mentors.

+

Diamonds *represent the physical world and correspond*
to the element of earth.

=

The suit of Diamonds highlights financial responsibility
and living within one's means. Consider how to be both
practical with your purchases and inventive with your
current possessions to create something from nothing.

NOTES

KING OF DIAMONDS

Generosity, happiness found in nature or spirituality

The King of Diamonds appreciates what he has but maintains a healthy perspective about the physical world and its limitations. Instead of feeling constrained, he shares his wealth and contributes to the greater good. He is trustworthy, and he knows that true happiness does not come from material things.

QUICK READING

Kings are rule-based and methodical leaders or mentors.

+

Diamonds represent the physical world and correspond to the element of earth.

=

This figure is reminiscent of a wooden Buddha, referencing Buddhist dharma and self-discipline. This card represents someone who has a clear perception of reality, reinforced here by the figure's meditative state.

NOTES

ACE OF HEARTS

Emotional, spiritual, or creative flow

The Ace of Hearts is about a state of flow that is overwhelming in a good way. A cup forms a fountain surrounded by water and fish. Here, the focus is on the active water rushing from the fountain, a forceful and steady flow of emotions and inspiration rising to the surface. It's important to nurture the Ace of Hearts flow when it appears. These moments are full of potential and inspiration but are fleeting and difficult to plan for or create.

QUICK READING

Ace/One signifies clarity and new beginnings.

+

Hearts represent emotion and intuition and correspond to the element of water.

=

Our "flow" could be any emotional experience that creates a sense of ease and clarity—times when work doesn't feel like work, when love feels all-consuming, or when spirituality creates a sense of well-being.

NOTES

TWO OF HEARTS ✳ TEMPERANCE

Balance, moderation

The angel here represents healing, patience, and guidance from a higher power. This patience allows for the thoughtful, balanced blending of the contents of both cups; change is within our control. To temper one thing with another is to create balance, to neutralize any negatives that come from leaning too heavily toward extremes.

QUICK READING

Two *signifies duality: a dialogue or a choice.*

+

Hearts *represent emotion and intuition and correspond to the element of water.*

=

It can be difficult to take the middle path rather than lean to one extreme or another. If aspects of our lives and relationships feel like too much, we can look for opposing actions to balance them.

NOTES

THREE OF HEARTS

A party or celebration

The simplest way to read the Three of Hearts is as a party, but
on a deeper level it is about friendship, platonic love, and shared
experience. It is a reminder to reconnect with people you care about.
This toast between friends could be a wish for health and good
fortune, an expression of congratulations, or a manifestation
of love and appreciation for being together.

QUICK READING

Three *signifies creation, as well as family or
group dynamics.*

+

Hearts *represent emotion and intuition and correspond
to the element of water.*

=

*The Three of Hearts is an outpouring of emotion shared
with family—biological or chosen. Celebrate victories
and accomplishments, especially the accomplishments
of the people close to you.*

NOTES

FOUR OF HEARTS

---

*Hesitation to try something new,
fear of repeating past mistakes*

We must often deal with disappointment before figuring out what
works. The Four of Hearts reminds us to remain open to new
possibilities rather than becoming wary or cynical. Flexibility and an
open mind are key to growth. A woman is offered a thriving flower
arrangement, but her perception is colored by her previous failures,
which appear in the foreground. She will be able to grow once she
honestly assesses what went wrong in the past.

QUICK READING

Four signifies stability, structure, and foundation.

+

Hearts represent emotion and intuition and correspond
to the element of water.

=

*Here, the stability of the number four could either
refer to contentment or complacency in relationships.
Movement and flow have ceased, so the situation
may be static and predictable.*

NOTES

FIVE OF HEARTS

Learning from mistakes, moving forward

The Five of Hearts is the "happy accidents" card. It is about viewing mistakes as tools for learning and growth. For better or for worse, things may not be going as planned. The three spilled cups support the growth of what's in the other two cups. A mistake has created something different—and possibly more beautiful—than what was originally planned.

QUICK READING

Five signifies imbalance and change.

+

Hearts represent emotion and intuition and correspond to the element of water.

=

Following the stability of the number four, the Five of Hearts introduces something unexpected—perhaps an emotional change. Maybe our feelings have changed, or we see a relationship in a new light. Unexpected problems may create surprising results.

NOTES

SIX OF HEARTS ✳ THE LOVERS

Love, beauty, union

This card signifies a meaningful, balanced relationship: one that makes us feel ready to face any obstacle. Whether the relationship lasts forever or for a short time, there is a feeling of destiny and wholeness to it. The shared center eye in this image represents The Lovers' shared vision. A healthy relationship can help us see the world in a unique way, perhaps better than we can see it on our own.

QUICK READING

Six *signifies cooperation, community, and communication.*

+

Hearts *represent emotion and intuition and correspond to the element of water.*

=

Caring and communication combine to create a sense of being "in it together." The Lovers represents a reciprocal partnership where each person gives and receives something in equal measure.

NOTES

SEVEN OF HEARTS

Secrets, imagination, new feelings

The Seven of Hearts represents positive and negative aspects of fantasy. From a distance, we may see an idealized version of something we want or an extreme version of something we fear. In either case, there is a sense of excitement and possibility surrounding the unknown. The cups represent choices, and their contents are for the reader to interpret. Some possible meanings include growth, beauty, or abundance (flowers); community or security (city); happiness (sun); wealth or vanity (jewelry); and danger or temptation (snake).

QUICK READING

Seven *signifies possibility, discovery, and spirituality.*

+

Hearts *represent emotion and intuition and correspond to the element of water.*

=

Seven is an active number and when combined with the suit of Hearts, the symbols embody freeform, directionless emotion. Here there is choice, possibility, imagination, and delusion.

NOTES

EIGHT OF HEARTS ✸ THE MOON

Subtlety, mystery, instinct

The moon is a symbol of mystery and receptivity. Unlike the sun and stars, the moon does not radiate light—its natural state is darkness. It is in a constant state of cyclical change and the phases we see depend on reflected light from the sun. It is tied to dreams, imagination, and the subconscious. This card asks us to embrace shadow and ambiguity and to let our emotions guide us.

QUICK READING

Eight *signifies patterns, cycles, and repetition.*

+

Hearts *represent emotion and intuition and correspond to the element of water.*

=

The Moon asks us to experience feelings fully and seek deep emotional truth. The phases of the moon suggest mutability, cycles, rituals, and the passage of time.

NOTES

NINE OF HEARTS

Selfishness, excess

Selfishness and excess may seem like negative qualities, but selfishness is sometimes necessary. Excess can also read as abundance. This card could also represent getting too much of what we wanted. We might think about sharing our wealth, responsibility, or feelings with others, so we don't become overwhelmed. Even if this abundance was earned, it may be too much to deal with alone.

QUICK READING

Nine signifies expectation and idealism.

+

Hearts represent emotion and intuition and correspond to the element of water.

=

The Nine of Hearts could refer to an outpouring of emotion that happens toward the end of a cycle. Sometimes it's necessary to let emotions out, even when it may feel selfish.

NOTES

TEN OF HEARTS ✳
THE WHEEL OF FORTUNE

Plans set in motion

The Wheel of Fortune is about life's ups and downs. Sometimes we're in control at the top of the wheel. Other times we're at the bottom. In early Italian tarot decks, the image of a King being crushed below the wheel functioned as a cautionary tale about pride. However, those historic decks failed to show that the wheel always turns again. The King is placed back at the top of the wheel, and the cycle continues.

QUICK READING

Ten signifies resolution and completion.

+

Hearts represent emotion and intuition and correspond to the element of water.

=

We may be at the end of an emotional cycle, but nothing is ever static. This card serves as a reminder that "what goes around comes around."

NOTES

JACK OF HEARTS

Unconscious thoughts coming to the surface, contemplation

A fish emerging from the water is a message brought to the surface from the depths of our unconscious. The symbol of the fountain indicates deep feelings that can no longer be contained below the ground and consequently make themselves visible. The Jack of Hearts is a carrier of intuitive messages. This card could indicate a need to trust our feelings and remain open to unexpected possibilities.

QUICK READING

Jacks are associated with inexperience; they are the students or apprentices of the deck.

+

Hearts represent emotion and intuition and correspond to the element of water.

=

This Jack is a dreamer, easily lost in their imagination. As a student of the suit of Hearts, they are learning to understand their emotions, intuition, and what bubbles below the surface.

NOTES

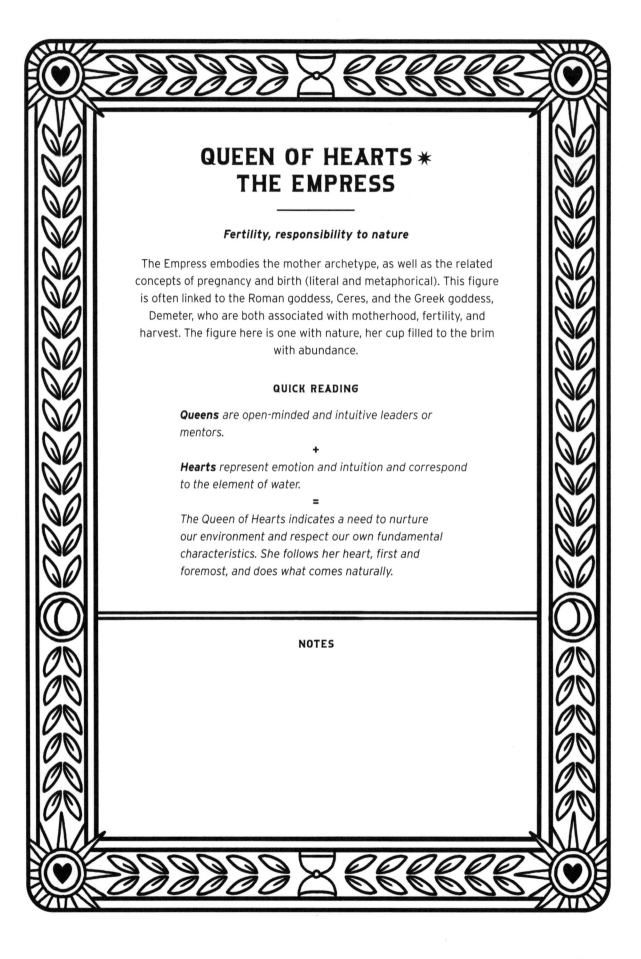

QUEEN OF HEARTS ✳ THE EMPRESS

Fertility, responsibility to nature

The Empress embodies the mother archetype, as well as the related concepts of pregnancy and birth (literal and metaphorical). This figure is often linked to the Roman goddess, Ceres, and the Greek goddess, Demeter, who are both associated with motherhood, fertility, and harvest. The figure here is one with nature, her cup filled to the brim with abundance.

QUICK READING

Queens are open-minded and intuitive leaders or mentors.

+

Hearts represent emotion and intuition and correspond to the element of water.

=

The Queen of Hearts indicates a need to nurture our environment and respect our own fundamental characteristics. She follows her heart, first and foremost, and does what comes naturally.

NOTES

KING OF HEARTS

Sensitivity and creativity channeled into professional success

This King rules with love and compassion and is a keen observer of the world. This card could signify someone who is artistic or scientific. This King confidently holds the ocean in his hands. It is filled with an array of interesting fish, which could perhaps represent dreams and imagination. The King of Hearts takes only what he really needs, knowing that his own survival depends on a healthy ecosystem.

QUICK READING

Kings *are rule-based and methodical leaders or mentors.*

+

Hearts *represent emotion and intuition and correspond to the element of water.*

=

The King of Hearts manages his own feelings and taps into others' emotions without becoming overwhelmed. He owes his success to the deep respect he has for the environment.

NOTES

ACE OF SPADES

Focus, clarity

The Ace of Spades encourages bold choices. The upright sword represents a belief in absolute truth. Imagine the sword cutting through all that is unnecessary to find the essential core. At the center of the sword is an eye in a triangle, reminiscent of the Masonic Eye of Providence. In this context, the all-seeing eye indicates support from the universe.

QUICK READING

Ace/One *signifies clarity and new beginnings.*

+

Spades *represent reason and intellect and correspond to the element of air.*

=

Life is full of gray areas, but the Ace of Spades represents absolutes: pure reason and intellect. This card brings with it the caveat that we should not become overly fixated on reason, ignoring our instincts.

NOTES

TWO OF SPADES ✴
THE HANGED MAN

Peace through self-discipline, freedom from distraction

The Hanged Man is one of the most spiritual cards in tarot. This card represents all that comes from practicing meditation, like peace of mind, a necessary break, and a feeling of connection to the universe. The focus here is on the figure's face and mind, rather than the body. They find peace by surrendering to gravity, both literally and figuratively.

QUICK READING

Two signifies duality: a dialogue or a choice.

+

Spades represent reason and intellect and correspond to the element of air.

=

The Two of Spades is associated with crossroads and in-between states. When making a decision, consider waiting it out, embracing that liminal space of uncertainty, and putting faith in the idea that a solution will present itself.

NOTES

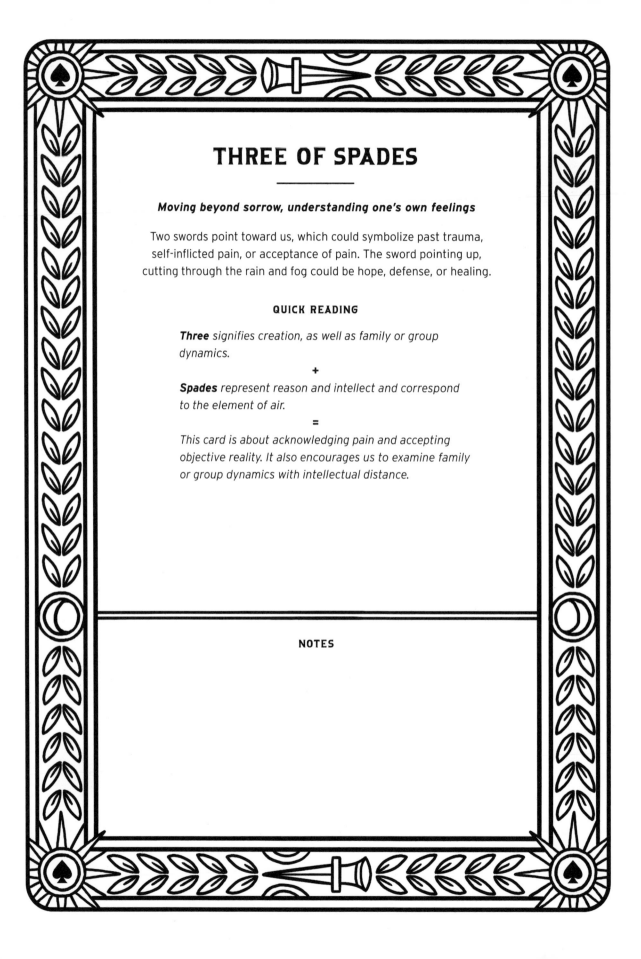

THREE OF SPADES

Moving beyond sorrow, understanding one's own feelings

Two swords point toward us, which could symbolize past trauma, self-inflicted pain, or acceptance of pain. The sword pointing up, cutting through the rain and fog could be hope, defense, or healing.

QUICK READING

Three signifies creation, as well as family or group dynamics.

+

Spades represent reason and intellect and correspond to the element of air.

=

This card is about acknowledging pain and accepting objective reality. It also encourages us to examine family or group dynamics with intellectual distance.

NOTES

FOUR OF SPADES ✳ DEATH

The cycle of creation, destruction, and renewal

Though it seems ominous on the surface, the Death card is primarily about change and renewal. Decay is necessary to fertilize new growth. The painted motifs on the skull evoke Mexico's Día de Muertos, a celebration of life and death. The holiday is an expression of love and remembrance for those who have died. The lilies wrapped around the skull symbolize new life after death.

QUICK READING

Four signifies stability, structure, and foundation.

+

Spades represent reason and intellect and correspond to the element of air.

=

Solitude and retreat are necessary to gather strength before the next phase in a cycle. Consider what phases or cycles are ending and what rest and recuperation might do for an inevitable rebirth.

NOTES

FIVE OF SPADES

Possible disappointment, a difficult opponent

When the Five of Spades comes up in a reading, we are slightly out of our depth. The illustration is from the perspective of the person who has folded their cards. No emotions are shown explicitly, giving the reader freedom to decide what the depicted defeat refers to and how much weight it has. Winning or losing does not always look the way we expect it to. A difficult opponent may be another person or circumstance, but it may also refer to an internal conflict.

QUICK READING

Five signifies imbalance and change.

+

Spades represent reason and intellect and correspond to the element of air.

=

Fives signify struggle, and since the suit is Spades, the struggle may be an intellectual one. Disappointment is not inevitable, but a challenge may yield an unexpected outcome.

NOTES

SIX OF SPADES

Leaving worries behind, a transition

The Six of Spades represents a passage from one place to another. The moon represents intuition, while the island signifies an unfamiliar destination. "The Six of Swords is a gate," Rachel Pollack writes in her influential *Seventy-Eight Degrees of Wisdom*. "Looking at it with sensitivity and then entering the picture will produce first a quieting effect on the mind and then later, slowly, a sense of movement within the self."

QUICK READING

Six signifies cooperation, community, and communication.

+

Spades represent reason and intellect and correspond to the element of air.

=

The Six of Spades signifies an intentional decision to move away from fear, grief, or difficult circumstances and toward easier communication, hope, and belonging.

NOTES

SEVEN OF SPADES ✳ THE CHARIOT

A triumph, a breakthrough, an inventive solution

The Chariot usually depicts a figure who is steering two creatures, one dark and one light. Sometimes horses, sphinxes, lions, or swans, these creatures represent opposing instincts being steered in the same direction by a strong will. Here, dark and light horses work together to escape their enclosure and run free.

QUICK READING

Seven *signifies possibility, discovery, and spirituality.*

+

Spades *represent reason and intellect and correspond to the element of air.*

=

The Seven of Spades encourages us to think outside the box to find creative solutions. It is a reminder to examine all possibilities and to incorporate all aspects of ourselves into our problem solving.

NOTES

EIGHT OF SPADES ✳ JUSTICE

Reason, fairness

Justice is about truth, balance, and objectivity. It is a reminder to distinguish between feeling and thought, action and understanding, intuition and evidence. The blindfolded figure references the classic depiction of Lady Justice, an impartial judge in pursuit of objective truth.

QUICK READING

Eight *signifies patterns, cycles, and repetition.*

+

Spades *represent reason and intellect and correspond to the element of air.*

=

The combination of repetition and reason conveys the idea of methodical examination. This card reminds us to take a step back and assess situations from multiple perspectives.

NOTES

NINE OF SPADES

The thoughts that keep a person awake,
a struggle to make sense of events

Imagine you wake up in the middle of the night worrying about something. That's precisely the feeling and concept embodied by the Nine of Spades. In moments like these, the stakes often feel higher than they are in reality. The positive aspect of this card is when we let anxiety-filled moments like these point us toward a fear worth confronting once we are (metaphorically) awake. Facing that fear can help put our concerns into perspective.

QUICK READING

Nine signifies expectation and idealism.

+

Spades represent reason and intellect and correspond to the element of air.

=

This card can signify a gap between perception and reality. Digging into our expectations and managing them may help decrease anxiety.

NOTES

TEN OF SPADES ✳ JUDGMENT

Waking up, an announcement

Judgment signals a time for making assessments, acknowledging truth, and taking responsibility. A rooster with ten sword-like feathers issues a startling wake-up call at the dawn of a new day. A new cycle begins.

QUICK READING

Ten *signifies resolution and completion.*

+

Spades *represent reason and intellect and correspond to the element of air.*

=

The Ten of Spades represents a reckoning of sorts. We set the stage for more meaningful beginnings after taking an honest look at the past, including our possible mistakes and the roles we played in them.

NOTES

JACK OF SPADES

Caution, potential

The Jack of Spades clutches their tarot deck and sword. They have all the necessary information to move forward but they hesitate to act. Their lack of experience causes doubts, and they fear commitment. This card can signal a need for caution or an overabundance of it. The wind is picking up, indicating that a storm is coming. There's little harm in being cautious, but soon a choice must be made.

QUICK READING

Jacks are associated with inexperience; they are the students or apprentices of the deck.

+

Spades represent reason and intellect and correspond to the element of air.

=

Elemental air is visible on this card, showing a strong wind that could change direction at any time. The potential for unexpected outcomes can create anxiety or uncertainty, especially in those who lack experience.

NOTES

QUEEN OF SPADES

Strategy, intelligence, ambition

This card embodies straightforwardness and bravery. The illustration, inspired by Joan of Arc, shows a warrior with unflappable conviction. She is willing to fight for what she believes in, no matter the consequences.

QUICK READING

Queens *are open-minded and intuitive leaders or mentors.*

+

Spades *represent reason and intellect and correspond to the element of air.*

=

The open-mindedness inherent in this court card unites with the intellect of the Spades in the form of strategy. The Queen of Spades tends to distance herself from emotional situations, but this provides perspective and an ability to make objective assessments.

NOTES

KING OF SPADES ✳ THE EMPEROR

Wisdom, experience, authority

In *The Pictorial Key to the Tarot,* A.E. Waite describes The Emperor as "embodied will," perhaps indicating a need to take charge and exert influence. If The Empress embodies the mother archetype, then the ram, a symbol of aggression and decision, captures the authoritative essence of the father archetype. The Emperor grips the sword and is ready to draw it at any moment.

QUICK READING

Kings are open-minded and intuitive leaders or mentors.

+

Spades represent reason and intellect and correspond to the element of air.

=

This card is the purest embodiment of authority in tarot, as it signifies both intellect and rules. The King of Spades can be a wise, fair, and trustworthy leader, or he can take on darker aspects of authority, such as the misuse of power.

NOTES

Published in the United States by Clarkson Potter/Publishers, an imprint of the
Crown Publishing Group, a division of Penguin Random House LLC, New York.

ClarksonPotter.com

CLARKSON POTTER is a trademark and POTTER with colophon is a registered
trademark of Penguin Random House LLC.

ISBN 978-0-593-57929-9

Printed in China

Editor: Sara Neville | Editorial assistant: Zoe Cramer
Designer: Jessie Kaye and Danielle Deschenes
Production editor: Sohayla Farman
Production manager: Luisa Francavilla
Compositors: Dix and Zoe Tokushige
Copyeditor: Sarah Etinas | Proofreader: Rebecca Zaharia
Marketer: Chloe Aryeh

10 9 8 7 6 5 4 3 2 1

First Edition